RESORT

and other poems

D0863354

Also by Patricia Hampl

WOMAN BEFORE AN AQUARIUM
A ROMANTIC EDUCATION

RESORT

and other poems

Patricia Hampl

HOUGHTON MIFFLIN COMPANY BOSTON

"Resort" appeared, in slightly different form,
in a limited edition published by Bookslinger Editions.

Copyright © 1983 by Patricia Hampl

All rights reserved. No part of this work may be reproduced
or transmitted in any form or by any means, electronic or
mechanical, including photocopying and recording, or by
any information storage or retrieval system, except as may
be expressly permitted by the 1976 Copyright Act or in
writing from the publisher. Requests for permission should
be addressed in writing to Houghton Mifflin Company,
2 Park Street, Boston, Massachusetts 02108.

Library of Congress Cataloging in Publication Data

Hampl, Patricia, date
    Resort and other poems.

    I. Title.
PS3558.A4575R44   1983   811'.54   83-10671
ISBN 0-395-34403-4
ISBN 0-395-34932-X (pbk.)

Printed in the United States of America

Q 10 9 8 7 6 5 4 3 2

ACKNOWLEDGMENTS

Certain poems in this book first appeared in the
following publications: *Antaeus*: "Hand, Eye";
Crazy Horse: "Hearth," "Last Letter," "Mozart
During a Snowstorm"; *Iowa Review*: "Blue Bottle,"
"Leading to Your Hands," "The Loon"; *Paris
Review*: "Tired of"; *Sing, Heavenly Muse*:
"Coldness."

Special thanks to Thomas Hart, my editor, and to
The Loft and the McKnight Foundation for a 1982
Loft / McKnight grant, which provided me with
a summer free to write.

For Phebe Hanson and Marly Rusoff

"The rose exceeds, the rose exceeds us all."

— ROETHKE

CONTENTS

CARO

RESORT 39

CARO

BEACH, BEACH HOUSE, AND SKY

Above, Orion is tilting
and the birds have stopped
being white. The fine brushes
of their feet leave marks
that mean nothing, though people
walk by, heads bent, reading closely.

Inside, the yellow flame of the oil lamp
sends flecks of light up its glass chimney.
The night is still, motionless as
this cup of cocoa, hot sugar
under the tight mauve skin.
A girl outside yells, *Run, run
for it, Eddie,* but the world
does not move, though maybe the sky does.

Beyond us, all of us, something
is happening. We haven't
the slightest idea. Today
the landlord came by to dig
for clams. I never have time,
he said, to dig for clams.
He frowned terribly:
he's still not digging for clams,
I thought. But there he was,
muddy, with a pail and shovel,
down on his knees
as you must be for this work.

DIRECTION

Being alone, write postcards
saying I love being alone.
Call it solitude,
mention the pleasure
of wasted time, the jolt
of red when you saw
the forked amaryllis
in the store window yesterday.
And your thought: if
I were happy
I would not notice this.

Dare things to change.
Well, they do, things do.
A flower pressed thin
as grit in the family Bible
becomes the color of ink
on an old agreement, broken,
no flower at all. There's too
much symbol in saved things.

The mail arrives, word
of a friend's death.
Pile your hair in a chignon,
sear your face with make-up,
for hours stare at the mirror
as if this were grief (this is).
You'll become beautiful
(the eyes get sad first)
and nobody will notice how
your hand rubs your temple.

Some ragged gesture,
the wound of too much explaining.
What you need is to stand still,
no mirror, no flower, no future.

HAND, EYE

Here is the salt in the shaker,
and there is the pink of the sunset.
No, here is the salt and rice
I put in the glass shaker
to keep the grains from clotting,
and there, across the electrical wires,
is the sky which contains
a drop of color that is spreading.
Or, here is the salt
(the salt *is* here — and the rice),
there is the sky (or sunset).
Here is white, here is
bone-white and star-white.
There is the shrimp of the sky
curled in the basket of wires.
Here is inside (warm).
Over there is outside (winter).
Here, naturally, is my hand,
what it can hold (salt
inside its window).
Here is nearby, hand, salt, rice, white,
what can be held.
No, looking up, here is the pink blur,
the other hand (not mine),
the huge cupped hand
showing its dark blue wires.
The salt is suddenly pink.
Later, not. Like my hand. Like here.

A DRIVE IN THE COUNTRY

All week with the pink neon slash
of the Flamingo Motel over my door,
all week the nonexistent flamingo
of Long Prairie, Minnesota,
the only bird, only hot light.
Then someone offers dinner, a drive
in the country. And we arrive at
the laid table of these broken fields,
the chased gold of stubble, dusk
stroked through the charcoal light,
a wine never fully finished.
I graze like any animal,
I am better now, sighing
at the gauzy pink of the sky
though the sun's last shout is clear.
In a moment we will be lost
in the hungry black line
out there, the solemn horizon
that, not grasping, grasps us.

EARLY TRAIN TO THE CLOISTERS

Another aspect of privilege:
to sleep late. 6 A.M. and the faces
are black, Hispanic, the oil
of first work. I'm going
to a gallery, my face is
a frieze of easy pastel.
For this moment we are together.
The conductor, announcing stops
on the loudspeaker, is gentle,
sane as a cool avenue, and black.
This public bedroom where we
catch our extra winks is
grubby as any dream, and intimate.
We're underground, then
we are in the air.
We didn't speak
and none of you knows this happened,
but as the doors shivered open
and you were gone to the dark day,
I wished you well, wished you sleep,
this face, this face, that.

THE WHITE

These are the moments
before snow, whole weeks before.
The rehearsals of milky November,
cloud constructions
when a warm day
lowers a drift of light
through the leafless angles
of the trees lining the streets.
Green is gone,
gold is gone.
The blue sky is
the clairvoyance of snow.
There is night
and a moon
but these facts
force the hand of the season:
from that black sky
the real and cold white
will begin to emerge.

MOZART DURING A SNOWSTORM

Hands are clapping in Vienna,
the child Mozart takes his bow.
Ladies reach for the triangular
iced cakes of intermission;
the small chapped Viennese hand
touches my forehead.

Snow is falling, snow
is falling in the twentieth century.
All the brief white threads sift
through the air like silence breathing
its own thin life between
the quick notes of the sonata.

The dense, heavy stars of afternoon
stud the brain with slowness.
We slam in iceboats across
our bleak landscape. We are going
backward, we are going forward,
history is a slick surface.

So much whiteness in one lifetime.
The children are shrill in the snow,
they are making a man.
A shovel scrapes like a thought.
In the bedroom a sheet is taut
across the double bed. We are like
everyone who has ever lived.

VIEWS FROM SEVERAL WINDOWS
for Nancy Rector and Terence Williams

Snow in the ridges of the tile roofs,
and wild hops frozen, sagging
like bad hair against
the telephone wires by the alley.

From the acute angle of the kitchen
the black door of a hayloft:
something that old, that useless —
except to the eye, which is
Victorian and pleased.

A streetlight winks on.
This happens almost a block away
and for many blocks; a strand
of yellow pearls knotted by snow,
by street and night.

This afternoon, sunlight manacled
the complicated hands of the winter trees.
Contortion was supplication.
Light clattered from the beseeching
bareness of the trees. It cut
the snow deeply. It rendered
certain trapezoids of snow black.

Below the living room window,
the intersection is marked,
two names hoisted on a pole:
Maiden Lane is east-west,
and north-south, Nina Street,
named for a whore.

Don't say whore,
say lady of the night,
say night
because it is dark and kindly.
Say night in respect
for that which, like all of us,
disappears.

THE GREEN OF EASTER EVE

The bouquet of sticks which is a tree
acquires a green, rounded
portion of sky, its own budding
cloud, people would say leaves,
bruised green there
a little more than the sky,
the recognizable shape
billowing with summer.

Out of sight
a few unsold lily plants
in the closed greenhouse
at the foot of the hill.
The lilies are risen
from the slick, bladey leaves.
Flesh so white
it is water, green
water hardly moving.

Night now
and the subject is black,
the wet street
is strict as a tap shoe,
the sky a hunched shoulder.
Parked cars lose their colors.
Only the oxidized umbrella
of the cathedral thrills
the sky, the whole mind.

The lights trained on the church
snap off. It is gone, hidden

like a thumb in a fist.
A few things survive —
sky, the edges of near buildings,
a dog the color of wood,
oddly accurate because
of the streetlight
he raises his leg to.
It rains and rain is green.

April unfurls in damp fronds.
Only the old hopes, the lilies
and the insomniac dog,
the romanesque vault hurling
its medieval miracle into
the foggy night.
And those two people
this afternoon in the slow,
splatting rain. Put your arms
around me, he said to her.
And opened his own, wide.

SUMMER OVERCAST

The trillium — or whatever this is —
is drenched, a pale bog bent on a stem.
The day is a sedge, and the sky
is very close, lowered and cheapened
like the ceiling in a rented room
where someone has gone to figure things out.
Somewhere the antique sky is unchipped,
a gilt-blue that people will pay and pay for:
Tinos, Mykonos, platters of Greek water,
plates of Aegean sun, the staccato of heat.
Here, the northern ledge of cold pewter
is slow, troubled (vagueness can be anguish).
Tea, poured, is smoky: what people in novels
drink staring out steamy windows, making decisions.
Buttered toast rests on a plate, framed,
possessing the sharp contours of loneliness.
The refrigerator kicks on as if it could give heat.
The listlessness of gray makes objects seem
emotional, capable of fugitive plots.
Outside, someone turns an ignition:
the isolated sound could make you sob.
But it's just a day, just a day.
The hysteria of adjectives is unnecessary.
It's a matter of tea, toast, a chair,
static on the radio, grasses moving
their plumey stalks, raspberries,
gooseberries, the month of July,
waves punishing the large rocks,
dinner at 7 (there's white wine),
a face in the wind,
a face calm in the wind.

LAST LETTER
for the poet James L. White

Everything is more beautiful today.
I'm sorry, it's not right when you're dead
for the first time this morning,
but the rain hits the black
asphalt like a hoofer, exhausted, heavy
under the transparent strokes of dance.
The pink geraniums (do you like pink?
                   I want to know if you like pink)
are hanging in a basket from the cafe awning
as dry as tissue paper on a package.

The lights of things have turned on
more intensely just now as yours
has clicked immaculately off.
The women at the next table are saying
something is cute, real cute.
One of them with earrings
the shape of hearts. *No way*
would I follow that oaf around
like she did — they're talking about love,
the only subject, darling,
except for this new one of yours.

Here's what I meant to do:
call you this weekend, go for
chicken salad sans at the Sky Room
and you'd whisper again the truth:
the really great waitresses
always chew gum. You approved
of their dismissal of us, charmed always
by any artist who couldn't be charmed.

You posed glamour
as the first honor of friendship
and we said darling
to each other like movie stars.
Your white, naughty smile:
Tell me again, Trish darling,
how we're going to claw
our way to the top.

The woman with the hearts at her ears
is saying that after 30 years of marriage
you can't expect . . .
and that the girl *wasn't* a gold-digger.
She says when you order prime rib
you just better not think
you're going to get it medium rare.
But the only words today
are endearments: darling, sweet angel one,
caro, caro (we liked to be affected
and spoke all languages for their flair).

Just this instant a cat streaked by outside,
wet and matted as carpeting in a vestibule.
His brown and black stripes were green in the rain.
A green cat, Jim, bet you never saw that.
And the hearts are gold, pressed tight against
each lobe, not hanging — in case you thought
I meant the hanging kind. No, pressed
like two kisses. And she's looking at the cat too.
She may be thinking about the cat
or about something else. I can't say for sure.

I'll keep describing things, getting the colors
right, taking down the dialogue, packing
the report with metaphor so it's art,
watching the world be unlikely and eccentric.
I call it honesty, as you do. But today
I call it keeping you alive just a little longer,
using the present tense though that's dishonest now,
and it is unholy, darling, to hold you
a second longer than you held on to us.

CHAMPAGNE
for Carla

Flutes, they call the glasses,
and we sat at our instruments,
statuesque as players
while the waiter poured the white foam.
It wasn't music, those bubbles
were intense as grit, sand-bits
flung on the roof of the mouth.
They burst open, Missouri geodes,
and sparkled, mica exposed on the tongue.
The sun was there on our skin,
the hills were green.
Turning thirty is a landmark,
you said, turning thirty.
And touched your hair absent-mindedly,
your early gray hair.
Your father drank, holding the narrow glass
like a pipe to be fitted somewhere.
Don't gulp, said his wife, who is not
your mother. And he gulped.
I can't see ten dollars for lunch, he said.
Trotsky, Whitman, Bunyan, Blake, the minds
he's dined with all these years.
But champagne! I cried, raising my flute,
burying Blake, burying the old radical,
the desire for champagne to be a tool,
your semi-mother next to your father,
the absence of the man you love,
burying it all — as if I could —
under the fine spray of sand,
under the sharp bits of glass
that broke in our mouths

in the sun
from the thin flutes
in our helpless hands.

half-life to his careful growth,
as she had. My womb was bitter, glad
for once to be empty of all that.

He carries heavy boxes
late at night, time and a half,
purchasing power, a yellow
bird of a car called Le Car.
He is an artist too: "I've been encouraged
to continue." Photographs,
one of her and me here last summer,
grinning next to Le Car,
blown up huge as the lily.
The foolishness of our simple affection,
magnified. The danger of examining
the beloved as she smiles
and stares out, inevitably,
from her own frame
into the disintegrating blue.

MY FRIEND AND HER SON TALK
BY THE SIDE OF THE LAKE

Their voices carry
but I've overheard nothing.
The morning air is crisp,
it chips the sentences like ice,
glittery flash of words,
the slow, melting water
of meaningless drops.
Or maybe they're saying
nothing that matters,
just the vacant pleasure
of being together.
The talking, food, two cups
of black coffee. The joy
of this blue place.

A year ago he told me,
"You think she cares?
She doesn't care.
I won a contest. She said, 'Oh good.' "
Bitter, bitter teenage beard,
brooding over the proud lips,
muttering their evidence.
He was buying her a Christmas present,
a picture of a lily, white,
over-lit, too innocent.
She loves you — what could I say,
the clerk there with her hand,
the oversize lily, the crowded boutique:
he'd never "talked" before.
She wants her own life. I said that too.
Said it as if I'd given my own

THIS IS HOW MEMORY WORKS

You are stepping off a train.
A wet blank night, the smell of cinders.
A gust of steam from the engine swirls
around the hem of your topcoat, around
the hand holding the brown leather valise,
the hand that, a moment ago, slicked back
the hair and then put on the fedora
in front of the mirror with the beveled
edges in the cherrywood compartment.

The girl standing on the platform
in the Forties dress
has curled her hair, she has
nylon stockings — no, silk stockings still.
Her shoulders are touchingly military,
squared by those shoulder pads
and a sweet faith in the Allies.
She is waiting for you.
She can be wearing a hat, if you like.

You see her first.
That's part of the beauty:
you get the pure, eager face,
the lyrical dress, the surprise.
You can have the steam,
the crowded depot, the camel's-hair coat,
real leather and brass clasps on the suitcase;
you can make the lights glow with
strange significance, and the black cars
that pass you are historical yet ordinary.

The girl is yours,
the flowery dress, the walk
to the streetcar, a fried egg sandwich
and a joke about Mussolini.
You can have it all:
you're in *that* world, the only way
you'll ever be there now, hired
for your silent hammer, to nail pictures
to the walls of this mansion
made of thinnest air.

BLUE BOTTLE

The blue-black flare at the bottom
of the red tulip. Inside,
the sticks of sex are alert and wet.
The eye of the penis
and its first glistening drop.
That's what happened
last night — not night
but the pink moment of dusk
when every eye, even the sky's,
sees clearly through the pastel motes
of daylight
into the navy steel of night.

Remember that cheap perfume
they used to sell in the dime store
next to the orange face powder?
Evening in Paris.
It came in a blue bottle
with a silver cap shaped like a star.
That's the blue I mean.
I twirled off the star
and smelled what was in there.
Sex was in there.
I drew that blue, bruised fragrance
deep into my nostrils.
I was at the cosmetic counter of T. G. Grant's
and my cousin had just explained
that the man puts *his* on *hers*
and "they have to line their breasts up too."
I wasn't afraid, no matter
how odd it was.
I drew in that heavy blue smell.

Much later I was afraid,
for many years I was afraid with you.
But last night
I looked at the small, sleepy
eye in the intelligent stalk.
The blue light was caught there.
I recognized it.
You I recognized.
I said, blunt as that eye and as innocent,
Your penis smells like the rest of you.
Star opened, flesh opened.
Night and the body
which are blue bottles
opened and opened.
It was the first day of spring,
the tulips which had been aloof
bent out of themselves,
blue night exposed.

LEADING TO YOUR HANDS

The blue Chinese carpet
in the hotel lobby
was the only place
I really wanted to make love.
In the *lobby?* (Your round, literal eyes.)
Not the carpet: the cobalt dragon,
his worsted cloud. Not the palms,
not the room or the clerk standing there,
asking for the first night
in advance if we didn't mind.

In the bar the female vocalist
had ash in her voice,
the Twenties in flint and drizzle.
Not an original voice, but Gershwin
died young again in her throat:
       the man I love,
       the man I love.

Our room smelled of hot showers,
vague damage. We made love there.
We slept. I heard you moan.
You said I spoke.
We're getting to know each other
was the complexion
you put on these things.

Then the walking, the city of slants.
The sidewalks were tall ladders.
We're tourists, you said, so we walk.
Also, we held hands.

In Chinatown we ate black noodles
and were insulted by the waiter
which we decided meant
he likes you, he really likes you.

On the cable car
you put your arm
around my shoulder.
It wasn't gorgeous or reassuring,
any of the things it might have been.
This was weight, burden ending
in the pitiless bloom of your hand.
I'm often depressed, you said, meaning
this is intimacy, the treasure
handed over, the soul tendered.
Others might say *I love you,*
but you wanted to give something
personal, something that sinks in.

It looked like this:
your arm across my shoulder,
a man touching a woman on a cable car,
casual affection, maybe long marriage,
unconscious gesture, tourism.
Wrist, knuckle,
the soft pads of the palm,
moony nails,
the straight-edge of each finger.

That's the life of desire.
But intimacy is this passing

back and forth of bitter news,
stale bulletins, accrued unhappiness,
the family's old gold.
What I wanted (I started this)
was your body. Forever, but
don't laugh.
Breathed fire was the idea,
wild animals, passion
I'd heard about or imagined.
But forget that, forget
the long story I was planning.
As usual, I oversimplified,
even though there was that good omen
we found together in the library:
the city directory from 1900
with our grandfathers' names
on the same page,
both marked Laborer.

COLDNESS

Last night the new snow lay glittering,
shavings of mica, unreal, individual,
more beautiful than snow, more cold.
We'll take a walk in this, I thought.
But you were already in bed
asleep; the new humidifier whirred
next to you in the dark.
The room was wet as a petal.

You lay curved under the blankets,
scooping for warmth.
I get cold, you told me one summer,
I get colder than other people,
it's from my childhood.
And there was a story about
a too-thin jacket and nobody
believing you, and wind and loneliness,
afternoons you sat reading
on the living room radiator.

Some nights when I get in bed
you say out of your sleep,
I'm cold.
And I tell you the truth:
your skin is hot, you're not cold.
Well, *you're* cold, you say and fall
asleep, sullen as a cube in a tray.

I never did believe
you got colder than other people.
And when you said you were hungry

the day we drove on the endless freeway,
I told you to *pretend*
you were eating a sandwich.
When you're hungry, you said,
we eat.

I'm afraid of sympathy
as if it were a collar, tightening.
But alone, I see you. Your body
last night was no more body than a curl
of cold butter on a bread plate.
It was hunched bitterly, silent
with regret, alone in our bed.

How beautiful then the accumulated
privacies of your sleeping face.
How glad I was that you slept
and did not have to love
this starry coldness
I had planned for you.

TIRED OF

Not the wrist of the sunset
which sinks every night
below the electrical wires.
That is pink, I'm not tired of pink.
But cover up the stars, the stars
are just the absence of clouds.
Let the clouds come, clouds
are vague.
Say you didn't betray me —
or am I being too clear again?
I'm a primary color
in your dreamy light.
On the windowsill a green jar
is filling with pink light.
I won't hate you, I won't love you.
There is the possibility of floating,
a pink cloud is scudding by.
And green is right here,
it is serenity
even though the color is bright
and, you said, much too obvious.

VENETIAN FOOD

A fog wandering like a pilgrim
held the city together our first night.
Pastel and crumble, bruised edges
of buildings, some blue neon (not much),
the violet heart of my heavy religion
I'd recognize anywhere.
The most arrived-at place of my life:
we stepped out of the terminal
and for once Europe was all there,
lapping water and temples.
That's a warehouse, sweetie, you said.
I was happy when you were the expert,
but I meant it: no need to show me
anything beyond the terminal.
I could see everything in advance,
like true love or a beautiful storm
moving in from the west, all
mixed up with good weather.

The fog made us Venetian,
being touched by what touched it.
We might have been that milky glass,
a dusty chandelier in the Fenice,
opera itself crowing away,
or the oily curlicues of squid
on a plate in a window, wearing
a severe corsage of lemon and seaweed.
For a moment, crossing it, I was a bridge,
not a famous one, small, leading
to a tearoom where the English were cozy
amongst their lacquered scones,

tea like Jamaican rum.
Then one of us was sweet coffee — you
it must have been — standing like sailors
at a zinc bar, cold, talking spaghetti
for dinner, talking art, talking
the Accademia has lousy lighting, can't
see a thing, talking language lessons,
talking coming back, for longer, a long time,
why not live here, why not?

A narrow apartment (dark canal, a rat
glimpsed would be OK), a gray cat,
a pot of those intense geraniums at our window.
Would we eat at home or in restaurants?
We'd eat at home *and* in restaurants:
the profound resolutions of fantasy, the wink
at choice. That trump always won
our bluffing hearts: for a moment
 we had everything. And fell
silent, in real Venice, tourist Venice,
the open Frommer guide on the table, lost.
We were Italian deep down like sun
that has spread on pavement all day,
all century, and before that, and after.

Together we broke the crusty bread
of dreams and unlived lives. We stared
into each other's eyes, mine dark where
anything can happen, yours blue
and all future. Stared and saw
language lessons, pure meals on white plates,

a fat neighbor lady with a tight apron
who doesn't like Americans but loves us,
forgives the War just a little because
we are learning her heartbreaker language
and her beautiful food. We stare
out of our own eyes, out of Venice.
This perfect arrangement
will never happen again.
We are eating at home
and we are eating in restaurants.
The lamp above the table is gold,
it is falling all over
with a litany of light
just as prayer does, the prayer
that bears no request in its shining.

HEARTH

You've seen those pictures
of the colonial hearth:
a black hook holding
the huge pot over the fire.
All the utensils were oversize,
the great wooden spoon as tall
as a woman in a starched cap,
the eternity of stirring.
I believe for a fact
the pot was never empty;
it never came off its hook,
why should it?
The hearth was huge,
a person could stand
inside the fireplace as if
it were a small hut, and warm.
Those people were smaller
than we can imagine,
we bend at their doorways.
In the dusty county museum
we hold their tiny, unreal shoes,
puckered like figs now
and not believable anymore.
We turn toward the hearth.
But what is the hearth
but a hook?

THE LOON

has four cries, one so manic
you shiver to hear it in the night,
beyond joy to plain crazy.
Another like grief, prophetic rage
that a child dies, or anyone.
And two cries in between,
but who bothers with those?
We go, most of us, for the grand gesture.

The morning could not be more frail,
gray as a pensioner's suit.
The huge lake rises in a drift
of haze slightly above itself.
Sun exists, but behind
clouds that are the sky.
An orange butterfly is too rich
but it is here: orange butterfly.

On 61, the Monson trucks plow
the asphalt to Canada.
Getting goods from one place to another
is as ancient as anything. Voyageurs
in canoes, the seventeenth century,
piles of pelts, tallow,
something dried for food;
there must have been coffee too.
Nothing's modern, not even need.

At Marge's cafe, the truckers are
lonely-hearts, they drink black coffee,
say they write music (just for fun),

want to go to Memphis. One has found
Jesus: I write about *Him* now — it saved
my marriage. On the formica counter
the kitchen-supply coffee mugs
already look like archaeology:
pottery of the region, once used as...
The hand holding the mug
will also become shard.
A future desolation claims these details,
and his voice, reaching for the breast
of the waitress, gave up years ago.

There must be a sound for all this.
Tires hiss on the highway.
A paddle was dipped in still water
and rasped the surface, the silence,
moving forward in a line.
Birds, startled by movement,
will make a low, grave noise
with their wings, and fly off.
These things happen at different times,
beyond one life. But with sounds,
with solemn cries and privacy,
doesn't everything finally add up?

RESORT

I 🦢

The point of this place: don't ask for much, ask
    for everything. Get: details, as everywhere.
July and the wild rose is the pink fact, repeated
    like a rumor in every corner of the fresh season.
Blue wedged in the interstices of pink and pallor,
    creating petal, petal, petal, more, more.
Five fast strokes of dampness on the highway where
    the whooshing trucks snap the tender green necks.
Five on the rocky Shore where a slick wave casts
    a spray of transparent pebbles against the pink tissue.
A yellow slur of pollen is exposed, all five muscles
    relax, open their fist, their body wide, wide open.

This is noticing, would fit on a postcard of a wave sent to T
    who sends back Polaroids of hollyhocks and overwrought
        city roses, proving he too is paying attention:
    Not thinking, just noticing. But he is a man gripping
        a dull brass bar in the corridor of a lurching train.
    A window is there, and a world beyond him, but there is
        too much salvation in the white steam, and the engine pants.
    Description — which is all we ever have to give each other —
        will not attend desperation.

Though girlish, these roses, flounces of a new dress,
    are no different (as girls are no different, as I am not):
        The cold brass is under my hand too,
    I stagger in the narrow aisle by the window
        as everyone presses by on peaceful business:
    First bell, second bell, all the orderly dinners
        of this weighty world.
Forgive me, my friends at home who count on breezy letters,

I believe the rose exists, though this description
        is lifted from memory. Worse: the desire for memory.
Forgive me, I believe eyesight exists
        though my mother has lost one eye
and the other is becoming milky as lost ambition.
        Forgive me, this faith is based on no miracles.
Seeing is believing.
        I hope to see. Just that. Just the rose.

The gooseberry leaves with their badly scissored edges
        are going yellow, already red in July, a bush
of permanent fall, the fruit blackened to mean winter,
        slim pickings, lean birds.
Also bluebells, husked from roots shallow in the glacial rock,
        dense-colored on their thin paper. But first,
accomplishing these flowers, rain.
        (It is a rainy summer, Mother, Marty, Terry,
Deborah, Jim, Al: my dears, written or not written.)
        A day of breakers, hard throws of water fizzed with spray,
hour after hour, so that any question, hurled or softly
        spoken, becomes mantra, becomes rhythm.
Any question, tossed wave, any whipped petal. Any. Mine:
        Why have I come here, why?

        ૐ

Did you come for the weather? Many do.
        For bad weather. I mean, because of.
You came with expectations?
        Always: I wanted to be great.
And now?
        Still.

Any other luggage?
I drove my car so I was able to bring a lot with me.
You thought this appropriate for a retreat — as you call it?
It is my nature to make a home. I used to feel guilty about this. Was made to feel.
But the cabin is furnished, is it not?
That's not what I mean.
Would you describe the cabin? You often call it your shack — is this accurate?

A fisherman's wife, in 1929, prevailed upon her husband — in early spring, I suppose — to build a few cottages along the Shore here. Egg money, her version. She wanted a Persian rug, a walnut bookcase with beveled glass windows, pretty things, extras impossible to explain to him. She also had a grocery store on the road. People stopped. There were honeymooners, hunters, I've heard whisky runners from Canada, but this she never suspected. She was Norwegian, Lutheran, a gardener. Is, rather: she is alive still. Her daughters run the place now: Mae and Junie, named for the first months of the tourist season.

Really?

No, but it's all right to make use of facts. In those years the highway was gravel. The cars rode high off the ground. Black cars, a cloud of sepia dust behind, nothing to call traffic. The women wore jodhpurs and tall lace-up boots. This wasn't sexy, but in the pictures it is, the way the past always is. The men wore suspenders. Lake Superior was as it is, roaring or silent.

Ah, history. But the cabin itself?

Is a shack.

A description of it?

I cannot provide. I don't know what it looks like. It is

something to look out of. A shelter. Has windows, has things
that are in a kitchen, also a bathroom, bed, table — why list
the invisible visible? I don't know the color: it is a shell I
am grateful for. Humble habitation.
But you like it?
It is myself.
How do you spend the day then?
I write. I'm writing now.
Without interruption?
Life is all one thing.
No visitors?
They come. I want none.
You believe you can live without others, without friends?
Never.
You might explain . . .
I write longer letters than anyone I know.
You said something about wanting to be great?
I'm afraid that . . .
A confusion of values. We won't pursue.
Thank you.
You have music, news — a radio?
Bubble-gum rock across the Lake from Michigan. And I
know they're going ahead with the neutron bomb. News
and weather and music. They arrive, but often don't apply.
World news — where is the world? Michigan weather —
this is Minnesota, almost Ontario. Mozart from Duluth is
full of static, angry, not himself.
Would you call it home, this faded resort — a last resort?
Home for me all summer, surrounded by other people's va-
cations, this strand of cabins by the big Lake. But have it
your way. Have the last word, last resort. Anyway.

44

II 𓅯

So, settled. Settled in. So, can fly.
    (Here, arrival is followed by the journey.)
Begin by sitting down, silent, a Russian in a novel
    who stops for a moment in a chair
        whether on the way to exile or vacation —
    the indistinguishable anguish of any embarkation.
        Not prayer, but close to prayer, closer than in years.
    The pause. The plunge, caesura between events.
        The knowledge we have, holding a letter,
    that reading between the lines is reading the lines,
        the terrible innocent white of what cannot be said.
    This is the blank space that must be lived, fitted
        between the dense fast paragraphs of every day.

Three destinations arrive together: the past, the present, future.
    Only the present is essential, we know.
        But it is impossible to believe this, although
    we have promised to pay attention, nothing else.
        Don't think, just notice! we remind each other
    on postcards (beautiful cards bought at museums
        where we have sought to train the eye: we send
    delicate glider planes, glossy tropical birds,
        things that move or sway subtly: a Cuban calla lily).

The past is always the reason for our sadness
    but never reason enough. We want misery to be richer.
We ransack the rose of this moment,
    we trespass the immaculate lawns of the future.
Does anyone leave well enough alone?
    What is my excuse? I am alone, and well enough.

I thieve this glinting day, the slash of carmine melon
    across the Lake where the sun will rise,
I cram it in the face of last winter, the year before,
    the dance 20 years ago when the awful red seeped
on the back of the white piqué dress. I go to the future
    for my mother's death, my father's. All this
to comfort the past-that-is-never-enough,
    that squalling baby never wished for;
to feed what cries to be fed, though
    it has had its fill, should sleep now;
to bandage tight the wound that needs only this blue air,
    to be unable to leave well enough alone,
to be incapable of the abstruse concept *well enough.*
    I go, as the mind goes, three ways at once, and splinter.

I beg forgiveness, I'm not sure for what: for confusion maybe.
    I pray, I am certain, for clarity.
        (This is a prayer then?)
    I will be well when a wave is just water.
        I have spent this first day on a rock, jutting wedge
    of the Precambrian age, so old it is not the past
        but permanence, fashioned. I have stared
    at the Lake, all day, all day, all-my-life-this-day.
        My faith is: this will help, will matter.
    There is a certain silence which is language.
        It swells, keeps time, like music, like passion.

    ತ♥

Something was wrong? Went wrong?
    My life broke in half.

You're sorry?

Sorry for myself.

You're looking for some sort of answer?

I thought I was supposed to furnish those.

Came here to find direction?

I'm contemporary under protest. Could we call it a rest, a rest before a new beginning?

Whatever you say. Was it love?

It was.

Ended badly?

I said my life broke in half.

You're of an age for that.

As people say when there has been a death.

Feel free to talk about it, won't you?

This is, all this.

But — forgive me — we can count on you not to go on and on?

What brevity there is in a wave and in the pigment of the rose! These are my subjects.

III 🦢

The rapt face of the full moon rises pocked and yet perfect
    from the far rim of the Lake. This is good,
        to look a heavenly body in the eye,
    the moony face, waxy with wonder,
        the bewildered acceptance we know in advance
is the only wisdom we're likely to get, no matter
    how hard we work. There is no work:
the world wobbles, as the moon knows, lifting
    itself from cloud to cloud, skimming
the gray tatters, getting lost, getting located
    in the swashy black of night.

I have coffee and a campfire, the long draw from a sweet cigarette,
    the props of loneliness, cold air, woolen shawl, bent shoulders.
Sight should begin at night, by glimmers faintly:
    the frail hand of darkness is kinder than health.
The sun, by day, is obvious and too helpful.
    It is crude, cuts the eye with its splintered-glass knife.
Give me instead this heavy island of the sky,
    the immense clot rising so near to hand,
larding the night with reassurance
    as if the night were a child
with a mother in a floating white gown
    who rushes down the dark corridor at the sound of a scream,
who stands by the eerie bed, who murmurs
    long, pointless stories leading toward
sleep and slow morning:
    and the night is such a child, and I am.

The moon never meant to awe us, to strike us silent.
    We're supposed to go mad: the boys in the next cabin know.

They flick the dial of their radio, blast the black,
    greet the huge transistor-face in her own frequency,
blare across the airwaves with the stricken sound
    of an acoustic guitar, the pedal steel's hard-edge cello:
        She's got a Mercedes-Benz,
        She's got lots of pretty, pretty boys,
        She calls them friends.

True, true, I want to call over to them, but I'm the only one
    listening to the words, attaching meaning as usual
as I stare into the sinking red and black fire.
    They are attaching their beautiful ragged cells to the night,
anything to crack the aggravating calm of the moon,
    the mom poised above us and rising.
They struggle at their blaze, wrathful with music.
    I am the single lady next door who reads,
who thinks sanity is the ability to write a paragraph:
    I go mad that old deft way.

I don't mind the noise and I'm glad they're drunk:
    beer is a howl for milk.
I don't mind the shattered silence. I like the music,
    and unwrap a stick of gum from its lunar silver,
chew, chew, my mouth snaps with sound, a salute
    from the silent side of the world
where spinsters brew their tisanes,
    imagining lust better than anyone.

Thanks for the noise, thanks for yelling *no shit,* for laughing,
    for the unsplit logs piled high that will never burn,

for the smoke, for the rising smoke, thanks. For
    never speaking to me, thanks for ignoring me,
my body sexless as a plank for a while yet,
    beyond you, beyond skin. Thanks, thanks.

I just hope when I choose to speak up, someone will listen.
    But I don't want to speak. Not yet. And not, probably, to you.
For once, I listen. You become moony over there,
    become music. You scream *Fuck you, fuck*
you, Frankie, you silly fucker, and you are part
    of the moon, the random part and rising.
Part of the moon that is leaving,
    that is smaller now (your fire is smoke,
mine orange embers: two ways of not giving light),
    part of the moon that is not intimate anymore, not
the insistent white face bent over our beds,
    but the aloof planet itself, cool and remote, as
every loved figure eventually becomes, and endless,
    part of the streaming that carries us forward,
that is our life, though we say
    good-bye every day and every night
until we become good-and-lonely and are all memory
    like history in some boring book
that puts us heavily to sleep.
    For we must sleep, must close our eyes
to see what this profound clock
    has trapped in its invisible hands for us.

Would you say you're a romantic?
    The moon means a lot to me, and flowers. "My love is like a

red, red rose" — this is what lovers should say. During sex
I hear the grassy sound of a bow pulled deep across a cello
— but nobody thinks I mean this literally.
But you do?
The chords of muscle, the horsehair and wood of passion.
Miss it? Miss sex?
I wake alarmed before sunrise. I seem to expect something,
but I can't focus. I never understand that it's sex. I pull the
curtain and the Lake is out there, vast metal. The light is
red and awful, just emerging in a line. It's beautiful but ex-
hausted like someone who tries too hard. I pull the curtain
and fall back, burrow under the blankets. It is a suicidal
moment.
You think of killing yourself?
I could never harm myself. No desire to.
But this talk of suicide?
Is a passive recognition, no plan. The waste of every urge
gathers in the smoothed flannel of the gray light. Short,
uncharacteristic stabs of hatred for existence. The sheets are
so cold they seem damp. There's a nasty laugh somewhere
between night and day which I cannot stop. So I want to
stop myself.
But you're never tempted to act on it?
Once I touched the scars, healed and harmless, on T's wrist.
The white lines from a razor blade, a decade old. I regarded
them coolly, the way a customer would inspect a small ob-
ject in a good shop.
Did you discuss it?
All the occasions we have to ask each other Why.
He responded?
"I guess," he said, so meditatively, "I guess it was a feeling

of utter hopelessness. Despair. I guess that's it — despair."
You were satisfied?
It was like the moment when the customer finally asks the cost of the fine, small object, and the clerk murmurs his outrageous figure. They both know the little white thing will stay right there: it belongs to nobody — certainly not to either of them.
He couldn't explain it further?
He says I know as much about suicide as he does.
You said the morning light, the toneless light, is suicidal. What's so awful about that?
The way a tuning fork sends out a stripped sound, gutted, and it isn't music. The real existence of light is arctic: it keeps returning to ice, to a severe transparency that frightens me.
Why frightened?
Before the sun starts winking, the morning is a dish of dry heaves. The equal values of light turn corners into centers, as if nothing were particular. Details cease to exist, and I lose my purpose: there is nothing to describe. The razor's white lines on an arm are the moment when nothing was as vivid as this blindspot of despair. It's a real moment, real as the rose.
Isn't the early gray light soft and lovely?
It belongs to dissolution.
Maybe you make too much of it?
At the Cross River Cafe Marge is baking blueberry pie and apple and coconut cream in this terrible light. She is fluting the pie crust in a decorative pattern. She jumps from bed to food, first meaning. "I don't even have time to look out the window till 9 a.m.," she says. Louie is drinking coffee at the

counter. He arrives before sunrise, holding on to a white mug. "OK," he says, "she left me, my wife left me, OK? But I got the kids, OK? Thank God for the kids." The survival savvy of work and love. But the life of attention is a stranger salvation. Looking is no way to survive the light.

You mean metaphorically?

Metaphor isn't the word for the white lines, it is the white lines. The lines of what cannot be said.

Why don't you sleep later, then?

I won't miss anything. Not even this.

IV 🦢

Draw away from the world — for the best reasons, trust me —
  and the world, creature of habit, rushes after, waves
    pursuing the dense privacy of this rocky Shore, reaching
  with glistening spray, joy that cannot contain
    itself, that should not, being joy, being waves.
Or maybe, the world is never gone,
  there is no away, no privacy or pursuit;
    the habit of attachment is never broken.
Relation arrives every morning in the tiny locked box:
  twirl the combination, secret rigamarole like a toy.
My puzzle is stacked in the wall with everybody's puzzle,
  this little town's roster of messages stored behind
  panes of glass like dry sandwiches in an automat.
    Friends appear in their tidy wrappers,
  envelopes too decorous to be our lives.
    Together the addresses form a hexagram,
  the occult calibrations of geography,
    my three lines unvaried at the center,
  the other three drifting at the top left corner,
    changing, making all the difference.
These are the believable oracles of friendship,
  carriers of chance wisdom and Chinese kindness:
    No Blame, No Blame, they say (and I say back).
We love each other, lines on paper,
  hearts on sleeves, kisses of plain prose.

Mother, first friend, this plump wallet of pages and newspaper clippings,
  cartoons (here's a laugh, honey) and the baleful horoscope
of Friday last (not that you should take it too seriously:
  Saturday was much more upbeat, but I can't *find* Saturday).

Her latest letter to the editor:
Are readers of the St. *Paul Pioneer Press* aware
that all reports from Northern Ireland come from
   English news services? Readers of the Mail Bag,
this writer trusts, will draw their own conclusions.
   Though frankly — penciled note in margin — I now
think I should have driven the point home. People
   don't read, they just don't.
Ah Mother, the black-Irish fret that makes
   you Jewish and trustworthy.

She sends the boy of my first French kiss; his death
   notice flutters to the floor, much smaller
than his tongue, not searching for anything
   anymore, not the eloquent rose I remember.
(You knew him, yes?
   Her ballpoint nose still sniffs my life.)
Worry grows like a right hand the left hand has learned to slap:
   I'm concerned about you up there alone.
      (I know I shouldn't say that.)
   When are you coming home?
      (Not that it's any of my business.)
She wants to talk to me — not that other people are unfeeling
   (that's not the right word).
The sex or relationship is not any criterion
   (that's not the right word)
for someone being a person you can talk to, someone who can help
   (even help isn't the right word)
and I'm not ashamed to say I cry sometimes because
   I miss my daughter so much
      (if missing is the right word).

Mother, alone in the pearl-cold morning, before
the sun puts its blade to the Lake, I break
with pride to be the daughter of the woman who searches
for the right word, who knows the word never exists,
whose courage is the hedgerow stamina of subject verb object.
Many days the Shore is Irish with fog
and the gulls' wings are oily as sweaters of newly carded wool.
This cottage industry of adjectives
is no big deal, Mother, as you know,
yet it's everything: you know that too.
The humble handwork of remote places finds
its few collectors, mostly other lacemakers going
blind in other cottages from their own formulations,
the bobbins we keep twirling. Like lace,
every word in the language is decorative:
I can't even promise to be necessary like silence
or plain cloth pebbly as oatmeal that people eat.
I crouch near silence to talk as fast as I can.

And yes, to get away. Away even from you,
my smokey revolutionary, my half-blind reader.
(Sorry, sorry the operation on the left eye
was not a success. Sorry I wasn't there.)
Distance is the hidden requirement of intimacy,
and my lips touch nobody's ear
though maybe these words do.
I want to say intimate things to everybody.
To you, Mother, and to you-who-is-everybody.
Here, I'm almost remote enough to be passionate.
A leaf must become strange, the rose unlikely,
and each wave is pronounced distinctly

like a foreign name, over and over — all this
so that one new sentence will emerge
out of the formal light of language,
the morning sun fresh on the nicked silver of a wave.

Don't worry, don't worry, I'll come home in September,
you know that. We'll go to lunch.
St. Paul will be Irish and Catholic and will claim me,
and you will
(if claim is the right word).

&

Is silence the main thing?
Two fighter jets from the Duluth air base just streaked
by. The sound is terrible, sometimes the boom is so loud,
we cover our ears. I've winced, waiting, as if we might be
bombed.
But the landscape is pure?
What old ideals we have!
But more pure than other places?
There is asbestos in the bright water. Marge's daughter
picked raspberries by the road and got sick, some weed
killer or insecticide.
The people are better?
Gossip is a jagged masonry, holding people together here as
everywhere.
You won't give any superlative to this place?
Love enters no contests.
Do you mean you are better here? Not the place but you?
Everything's in place, everything's the same. Not a grudge

is missing. I just float more here. I have fewer gestures. I am a student.

Your teacher?

The rose, the lessons of unfolding.

So it is a matter of silence?

The rustle of petals and of the wind. The relation of the rose to long sentences.

Embarrassed by so much talk?

The rose has one job; this is another. Admire the rose; forgive my own unrefined face in the wind.

V ﾚﾟ

The Lake today is a French watercolor drizzled
    with a blue not yet dry.
Gulls float near the Shore, snub two-tone swans
    in the mammoth formal pool of midcontinent.
Or some of them fly, darts describing pure arcs
    without the troubled ambition of a target.
Then, out of the casual trajectory, a lunge, a grab:
    sharp hunters of meat after all, business in their beauty.

Pastel, all shimmer, rises from the water, becomes sky,
    reaches the goldenrod's matte yellow on the Shore,
then finishes its vague philosophy of oneness
    with the lavender syllogism of the aster.
Pastel rises from the sea, as life first did, the route of everything,
    out of the wet depths, floating up, not digging out.

Never imagine effort: change is a floating figure,
    pastel rising, a mermaid dripping water, drenched,
water streaming from the runnels of the eyes, down
    the fresh features, tears which course down
the reclusive face of the past, its grimace of regret and anger
    finally stirring from dangerous privacy,
reaching for the extended hand of dry land where
    all the flowers are, the rose's faded fist of pink.

Here are tears, here (you hope) the secret springs of bliss,
    the buoyancy of unexpected sobs, life rising to the surface
from a fissure in the stony coldness of good intentions,
    the first burble of turquoise gushing up
like the headache of spring, the clot of desire finally moving,
    clearing the blank air with color.

Tears are the genuine transparencies of the past,
   round cameras of remembrance that can't be ripped up.
The times in bed, holding each other in the grainy light,
   saying *it doesn't matter, it doesn't matter,*
the fat album of forgivenesses
   that might have assured the future, but did not.

Cry and be blue, that jazzy color of feeling.
   Cry for the past, hands held at the dinner table,
a whole meal of lost love, the baffling longevity of jokes,
   the way nothing ends when you say the end.
The camera keeps shooting, shooting,
   and you become blind from so much sight.
The little religion of noticing, fresh as fanaticism,
   underestimates the old icons of memory.

The beautiful mermaid of change rises weeping
   and cannot explain herself, voiceless in the sung liturgy of loss.
We do what we must do, never knowing why,
   saying *and that is that, that is that,* the amens
of whatever prayers there are in rhythmic phrases,
   the half-step above sobs, innocent of requests.

Change is a season's only commodity,
   and no disappearance has the entirety of summer's,
the outrageous miracle of September's red leaves.
   July works hard, a laborer stoking the rose's pink boiler,
the hissing effort of worker bees alive beyond loveliness,
   intent on the manufacture of food.
This is the beguiling exactitude of the world in progress,
   but our change is clear tears, no bright tricks, no rose.

Sob aloud *I'm so sad, I'm so sad,* words of water.
   Like any wave, this voice repeats and crashes,
reduced to sound, meaningless spray of short syllables:
   so sad, so sad, so sad, oh my god so sad.
It is impossible to speak the mother tongue of misery;
   the loss in translation is the loss of pain, first integrity.

The cabin wall is marbled with a reflection of watery light.
   The eye, poor fool, can't help itself, quickens with interest,
converted against its will, anchorite of attention.
   Despair is real and remorse: abstract and strict as terror.
But the ornamental soul of the universe has a tendency
   to be fascinating, and uses the trade secrets of the season.
The light winks on the pale green ceiling, the light
   is the whisper of sun and Lake, accurate as no feeling can be,
a lesser rainbow in this summer without rainbows.
   It is something to regard, the played hand of the sun,
all aces on the green wall, no bluff.
   The agates on the Shore are potential gems,
the clouds are cunning sculptures that move,
   and this black and yellow bee has been upholstered badly.
No denial on earth, no sob, can stop the flower market
   of late July, the bazaar where we buy and sell beyond sadness.

Hours away, my mother holds her hand over one eye
   (the surgeon bungled the operation, but sent the bill)
reading as best she can about the Belfast riots.
   Her faith has nothing to do with what she sees,
her religion is racial and furious: garlands of grudges
   hang from every Irish starvation and Maze Prison
is no maze to her: an English form of gardening, all hedgerows.

I'm all for despair: my own mess and the lost causes
  of her eyesight and the Irish language.
But I can read, I can read, she says, demonstrating
  her system of patches and eyedrops.
And there are whole villages where Gaelic is still spoken:
  you're ignorant of the facts, honey, face it.
She sees everything there is to see. Her reports,
  as readers of the Mail Bag know, are succinct
as a sucked lemon and ask no special favors: I trust you
  to draw your own conclusions, dear reader.
This is the blind trust of real eyesight: things will be OK.
  I'm here by the big water, here to take the waters.
Mine also is a visual complaint: I must see the rose,
  then say so, then go home.

Summer, shrewd doctor, treats the eye before all else,
  sends in the season's tray of soft foods, pollen and rose,
the liquid of light coming through the window's glass straw.
  There's nothing to do but rest, float, heal by changing.
Though the chart at the foot of the bed is marked Quiet! In Great Pain!
  the green light is cracking gold jokes and it does not hurt to laugh.

       ह॰

How long have you been here now?
  All of July, first of August.
Feeling better?
  I can't complain.
What's all this?
  This is the description of a complaint, not a complaint.
What is healing?
  My eyes. I stared too long at myself.

And now?
  I do the eye exercises of the world.
What do you see?
  The rose.
But they're gone now.
  The whole rose, the whole life. Keep looking.

VI ॐ

July's shutter has clicked, light spreads itself
    on the folded water, and summer gets serious.
This isn't a portrait of pastel anymore:
    color thickens; leaves darken like thoughts held too long.
Last week the birds drilled the citrus of the gooseberries
    but now the beads on the branches are deep as an eggplant.
Here, summer is never the business of heat:
    the Lake is a pan of cold water set before a fan
and summer radiates an arctic intelligence.
    Light ripens, the science of longing moves forward.

But how cool and steady the lives of leaves,
    the narrow canoe of the mountain ash, the open paw of the maple.
Imagine a single thought your whole life long
    in the shroudy monastery of maturation.
Imagine thinking nothing bad was happening to you
    though you lived the usual tragedy: emerge, grow, darken, die.
Imagine never trying to avoid pain
    (I've been guilty of trying to get out of this alive).

In the end, we want something practical from it all,
    this much knowledge for this much anguish;
but all they carry in this grocery store is certain articles of faith,
    certain cool green leaves that waver, that stand silent.
How I'd love to cut the fine talk and just be handed the groceries:
    a bruised apple, a dented can of soup, lettuce
the stockboy pitched on the dumpster behind the supermarket,
    the generous gift of waste scavengers seek in lost places.
Here, off the fireroad by the old town dump,
    the wild raspberries are going bad already
in the cloudy jelly of their ripeness.
    Nothing is perfect except the light falling on imperfection.

Here I am, imperfect, the August light falling on me,
   picking raspberries to save my soul.
The panting life of greed finally gets its chance;
   summer agrees to be touched, taken.
That's how it is: looking has become a firm grasp.
   If you want something, shouldn't you be able to have it?
Oh, it's not that simple: you have to take it,
   you have to straddle this sandy clump, reach down,
grab under the stunted leaves, get the red thing you're after,
   dump it in the plastic bucket

And move on, move on. There is so much to gather
   and who picks just one raspberry in this clump, this life?
There is a lot to notice: not just the steady progress
   of leaves down their serene corridors, not
only the water shifting its meaning every minute,
   not the rose, pink moth that fluttered and is gone,
not the refrigerator, dumped here seasons ago,
   standing bulky as a head nurse overseeing the situation.
Light is everywhere, spilling, creating its opposite.
   The real noticing is random, like love's choices,

Like thought. It darts from a leaf to a century,
   from this light grazing the water to the sudden slash
of your face, remembered, more beautiful than it's supposed to be
   after all this time, after everything that happened.
I keep reaching, but every thought looks the same in the bucket,
   every memory catches the light.
There's no way to forget the past — I know, this I know,
   but why are the darts of feeling so quick
to sliver the eye? Someone was taking pictures secretly
   for years — a monster of precision intent

On the exacting art form of happiness. It's all laid out
    and I must turn the album pages.
I've noticed the days turning, the minute season of each day
    spinning through its crop of details. July was all urge
and I, divested of any particular life, was all eyes.
    Summer, virtuoso of longing, has been my passion.
So put away the old felt album, all those pictures
    taken by a breathless voyeur, those film classics
that keep coming back and back. Did memory ever make
    a movie that didn't make you cry?
And I'll cry every time; they know how to do that to you,
    but that doesn't make it art.

There was no way to gather the rose, no purpose
    to plucking every one, no plastic bucketful of petals.
No way to get the thing you really want. The season moves on
    and August is sweaty away from the Lake by the raspberries,
right here by myself where I'm trying to start civilization
    all over again, humbly: the hunting and gathering stage,
right here where faith is just one little red plush button
    after another, where repetition is innocent,
and the only advice humming in the swarming light is
    gather it in, gather it all in.

Are you looking for a different life?
    A *different past.*
Consisting of?
    The absence of various particulars, certain screams, a cata-
    logue of silences, whole chapters of malice.

The elimination of certain people?

*The clouds, shipping their cargo of shapes, form and re-form
the faces of vapor. I want everyone intact; every face in-
evitable, essential.*

But the events?

*All right, if that's the way it is; I'll keep the ruthless plots,
the badly written paragraphs that fit no finished story, the
occasional lyric lines that seemed to promise so much. I'll
keep the whole business.*

That's a life plan?

*It's meant to be a small work of history. Later, if I'm lucky,
I hope to take up architecture.*

You want to make something? Something grand?

A house, a garden. What you would call a different life.

The old willful life of happiness?

*I sense I'm supposed to experience disappointment; that's
how I'm to learn to be interested.*

Interested in what?

*The faces that form and re-form, the delicacy of each imper-
fect shape, the flawed angles of a petal.*

You think that's bravery — looking at a flower and calling it a
person, calling it the ragged past?

*Eyesight starts where the light is kindest. Here is one face,
call it the rose, call it cloud or ripe berry. Work by degrees
to the sharp beam of his face, her face, telling me how it
was. Work to my face saying, yes, and yes, and yes, my
dears.*

VII 🦢

August's dense astronomy fits itself, all stars,
    into the sky's black observatory.
Nothing is solitary up there, nothing is a moon.
    Lying flat on a boulder at the side of the Lake,
I am one edge of things, the sky the other.
    The stars take shallow breaths and burn.

Heaven can't sit still all year: tonight
    the motionless dots dart with electronic brevity
between the fixed white stones of the other stars.
    Are they dying? They betray themselves, shift
their moon-colored light three inches, three light-years.
    Maybe luck exists, maybe I will betray myself;
a declaration of the changing heart could flare, fade, leave things
    looking harmless after all, just as these

Glancing minnows of the summer sky do: a star
    spurts and disappears. Death without loss.
I keep wanting something big to happen, but painlessly.
    I'd cheat any way I could, if I knew how.
But the random light of change, casual, soundless,
    happens and happens. Everything is remote,

Even my back against this rock is anonymous, all bone,
    although bodies have sloping curves meaning touch me.
The damp strokes of the shooting stars splash, send
    a rain that never arrives. I'm safe in contemplation,
no thorns in the white torn petals above,
    no thoughts, only memories.
Something happened a long time ago —
    What was it? Who made me so happy I was full of stars?

It is my father, standing by me again on the screened porch
    (easy tonight to flare delicately to his side,
the motivation of years is swift as these stars).
    It is raining, Dad, all those St. Paul summer nights.
The street is a stone floor, we agree, beneath a cathedral vault
    of elms, sooty from night and our idea of religion.

A moment ago we were in the living room, Mother was reading
    herself into her furious Irish elegy (Parnell is dead, dead).
Peter was placing a decal on the lacquered wing of a model plane,
    his tweezer poised, a passion for small, sane moves.
They are behind us still, wavering in the skim-milk glow of the Magnavox
    while we are drawn, strange moths, away from the light
to the wet fire of rain. How we love the thirsty communication
    of clumps of dirt and heavy air, you and I, you and I.

Your hands are in your pockets. I'm next to you, girlish
    and electric, all my talk talk talk. You're silent
enough for both of us, a man who grows roses for a living, wearing
    the mouse-smile of a listener though not necessarily listening
to me: some joke from 1937 you never quite got, some
    greenhouse crop to worry. I chatter, am distant as a star,

Which is how you love me, though sometimes you put
    your hand on my shoulder, a gesture
so affectionate it is unwilled, unaware of itself:
    I am unlikely but yours.
We are animals and have caught the scent of rain.
    Or we are even more subtle, we are roses
and lift our burdened heads on the tender necks;
    we see the first random dash come carelessly down,

A splayed particle of the night sky, tentative and large,
    less targeted than the rapid fire that follows,
the plain rain that puts on a show,
    a fast dance, I tell you.
Doesn't the rain look just like ballerinas, Dad?
    (I'm all for metaphor.)
The ricochet of rain on the black street makes
    little tulle skirts (I'm telling you) with tiny legs on point.

Can't you, can't you see them, the ballerinas? (The strident voice
    of women comes from wanting the world to be lyrical.)
How silent you have always been, waiting for
    something big, not money (though money is a flower,
it opens bright and wide), not the greeting
    of the bank president (you admitted

You were pleased — that suit cost $400, easy),
    not the satisfaction of important work (in the hospital,
after your first heart attack, scared and humble, saying
    if a guy'd been a doctor or *done* something . . .).
What you wait for has no name, though I keep insisting:
    Doesn't the rain look like ballerinas?
Every wet summer night we stand here, every night I gush
    my metaphor, every time you say

The true word, patient integrity of eyesight:
    No, you say, it doesn't look like ballerinas.
Not bothering to argue, just saying
    No, most fatherly of words, saying No
so that it can be dark and raining — just raining,
    so that somebody around here is telling the truth.

So that twenty years later I lie on my back alone
    and say *alone,* so that I regard the stars
saying nothing more complicated than *stars.*
    You didn't just grow roses, you sold them —
such an unlikely thing to do with a rose.
    Is that what honesty is, knowing the soul of the world is economic?
Then, Dad, what is freedom? Your hand is on my shoulder,
    the night is slivered with stars.

I'm supposed to say something,
    that's why I'm here.
I get scared if things get too simple:
    The safety of ornamentation is what I trust.
But maybe that's what you meant: don't describe things,
    just call them by their names: star, rain, rose.

     ಎ🌿

Does history change things?
    Not feelings.
But something is changed?
    Seeing is.
How?
    *A fisherman's wife, an immigrant, used to look from this
    Shore out to the Lake. Her husband was out there some-
    where, lurching. She couldn't see him, or safety.*
What did she see?
    *Norway and death. But she never said death; she said high
    waves. She said a good catch. Herring were silver pieces.*

What do you see?

Sixty extra years. And the Lake — if we must call it a lake (it is steep and drowns like a sea).

What else?

I see what I imagine of others — people on vacation (a working man's coastal holiday), resting near heavy industry; the taconite plant is a churning lighthouse, the iron-ore boats, strung with safety lanterns, look like cruise ships at night, as if people danced and whispered lovely lies on deck, twirling. And I told you — I see the fisherman's wife (he died in his bed at 85). I see my imagination: it makes me sad.

Why?

It is the soul of inaccuracy.

A crude definition.

Just a fear of myself. I see things clearly, but what if they never happened?

So what?

I don't want to make things up. I just want to make things.

How is that done?

The rose happens by degrees, but the seed is a bundle of firm assumptions. Form unfurls. Construction is an unclenched fist.

You're still talking about pretty flowers?

I understood all along the urge behind the blossom — who doesn't? Withering is the mystery.

What happens after the blossom, then?

Something adult happens. I don't know what to call it.

But you must call it — call it something.

I won't call it maturity. And death's too solemn.

There is a name for it, though?
 There is always a name.
So, after the blossom?
 Comes usefulness.

VIII &

Across the Lake: lightning and the future of frost.
  Winter does not depart, even in green August.
    The restlessness of rain and this sensation
  I refuse to call loneliness send me to
      public formica and coffee wrung from
  a whining machine like a choked confession,
      the Morning, Morning, Morning, when I take my place,
  and am reassembled by the tools of greeting.
      For an hour I sit amid society, the whispering cafe
  by the Cross River waterfall where the windows filter
      the hazy light in slanted sheets, as underwater.

Outside, the white sign next to the rushing river
  is cautionary as an old fiction:
      Slippery Rocks, Dangerous Falls,
        Lives Have Been Lost Here.
The cafe is all these pools of moving water,
  familiar rush toward one another,
      the gush of gossip, that misunderstood art form,
  the courtesy which is weather endlessly considered,
      the local history of sleet sought in sipped coffee.

Cancer is always good for a murmur, a hush,
  someone young, with three babies
      (but there's a chance, there's always a chance).
  She was gray as a wick and as thin, buying
      diapers at Zup's, laughing too.
  She wore a wig, wasn't it a wig?
      Treat me normal, that's what she says.

Inspiration comes from living hard, the slapped wife
  who finally got smart, whose husband remarried:

A slut, just what I would have wished for him.
A policy of no regrets and laughter,
    I am what I am: Give me the blueberry pie
and put some ice cream on it,
    who cares?

Young men, slumped beautifully in blue jeans, try
    to ward off the future by recognizing its ambushes,
        but the female voice is notched above their ears.
They devise systems, warnings, buzzers, lights: "See,
    I've noticed this, My name is Mike, your name is Tom,
but they call you Michael, they call you Thomas,
    they mean business, they mean marriage.
Like she said, Want to go to the movies, Michael.
    Shit — this I've noticed over and over."

He slopes bewildered against the soft tumble
    of a voice that is all pillows, a violet color
        he'd give anything to locate once and for all
because its soul, he knows, is shiny as a toaster.
    "You got a point, you got a point,
I never thought of that." But his friend
    is poised delicately away, just waiting
for his own full name to be spoken
    deep in his ear and private.

My money clicks against the saucer. I haven't opened
    my mouth except for this hot coffee.
        I'm all ears that hear half-sentences
and the bray of a joke in the corner. Everything I want
    to know is whispered and I can't get close enough to anybody.

Along the Shore, the water stammers against the rocks
and the lightning is blue as a tram wire across the Lake,
bruising the sky a lavender girls love for dresses.
It is August and the roses are nothing
but green leaves and these flimsy nails
that don't hold anything together.
There is red in the thorn's polished
horn but nowhere else, no red.

Home through the abandoned resort, Star of the North,
named for something lost in the sky. I sniff
the char from a cabin burned down last summer,
the sooty affinity of rain for old fires.
Bachelor's buttons and chives rise
in clumps by the blackened heap.

How white the daisies are above their fuzzy stems
and the fiery paintbrush oozes foam like a mad dog.
Color today is the contortion of light
and nothing seems as accurate as gray.
I walk in a fog, though there is no fog.
My arms catch in spiderwebs slung like barely woven sheets
between the creaking firs, the filmy
gray of a ghostly laundry.
I sweep the thin knots of spiderweb from my face
and keep going, keep going.

The butterflies are black, a chaplet of white
draped on the solemn wings. They bow as they move.
The severity of the day is chalk on the blackboard
of all these lives, the black formica
where my arms rested, the dark green voice

trembling all over from violets and hidden silver,
    the wig of blond curls that is uncaught cancer and courage.

This year the stems of the thimbleberries are big with goiters
    and nobody can explain why, nor why
        the blueberries are abundant, the raspberries gray,
    the black flies lacking the desire for anyone's ankles,
        the sky empty of rainbows.
This day is rain and the promise of rain:
    more mystery, more low murmurs together
        over what we walk through, the frail webs
    we never understand though they catch
        at our bodies, straying over a jacket
    and are damp to the touch, though
        they are strong enough to muffle a buzz forever,
    the tidy bundle of a fly, packaged outside my window
        as I watched, as I rubbed sleep from my eyes,
    as I determined once again to see,
        to see even though it is dripping rain
    and gray is the proclamation of sleep and cocoons,
        the slick lichen on the rocks where lives are lost.

      ै॰

What do you see?
    The same.
Tired of describing?
    Things are becoming very simple.
What do you feel?
    It's getting cold. I'm wearing a sweater.
What do you think?
    It's almost time to go home.
And what do you know?

IX &

The deluxe loneliness of September is here, slinking
    furs of fog, an ensemble punctuated by sapphires,
those few days more rash than the meridian of July,
    color-fast and glassy with light.
A whole month supported by the inherited gold of summer,
    the glamorous bright season.

The air is mushrooms and old heat, a stew of leaves
    and the shelled blossom-ends of raspberries.
Blueberries, by the railroad track, are black, reserved
    as shoes under the leggy foliage.
Some leaves are construction paper, some
    plastic gels dropped on the ground.

The rose was summer, the girlish flutter of pink,
    brazen pollen underneath it all, or I'd thought
it was the dead tongue of my first love, something
    romantic and vague slipping into sad green, past blossom.
But it is September, first frost, and the rose
    is a vegetable, practical as a widow, the stuff
of tea and a jam you buy in a health food store.
    Rose hips are more rose than the rose, more pink,
the jolly late apples of all that lyricism.
    The frank body of the flower unfolds its heart
which is pelvic, most beautiful bone,
    perfect gesture.

Never pick rose hips until after first frost:
    this rule you have observed. Now, the grass outside
the shack is crusted with the first lichen of frost.

Now go ahead, harvest the rosy buttons, all
their lives packed into the shiny pouches. Inside,
   their pulp is orange as the season, the fire
that resides in every ripe, ready thing. Inside
   is the food, something useful.
What you were waiting for, what you kept touching,
   what you meant to say, meant to confide,
what your mother bears as her Celtic grudge,
   what the summer released, what each letter in the box
had as its further address, what the rose reveals,
   not rose, but rapture.